GOODBYE, FEAR

The Goodbye Series #4

TAMBEARA WATKINS

WATKINS CHRISTIAN PUBLISHING

Tambeara Watkins / Watkins Christian Publishing an imprint of Leaf Stone Publishing

www.leafstonepublishing.com

"Scripture quotations are from the ESV Bible (The Holy Bible, English Standard Version), copyright © 2001 by Crossway Bibles, a publishing ministry of Good News Publishers. Used by permission. All rights reserved."

Goodbye Fear/ Tambeara Watkins. -- 1st ed.
ISBN9781701908697

ii

ACKNOWLEDGMENTS

Thank you to all my readers and my family for your support.

FEAR

This is a story of a mother, her son, and generational fear.

The son leaves his home at 6:55 am, hops into the truck, and arrives at 7 am at his mom's house for their morning coffee together and a dose of fear before he would leave for work daily. This morning he drove two minutes but was stopped by slower traffic before reaching his mom's house. He knew that he would be late and thought nothing of it until he pulled into the driveway and knocked twice as mom requested before entering the home with his key. He walked into the house and called out "mom," but there was no answer.

It was 7:05 am, and the aroma of freshly brewed coffee, two mugs, sugar, and cream on the side sat at the dining room table. But his mom was nowhere to be found.

He called out again. "Mom, where are you?" she usually met him at the door with news of fear for the day. No answer, his heartbeat faster at the thought of something happening to his mom. He raced in and out of each room, calling out, "Mom, Mom" Oh no, what has happened to my sweet mom? he thought." Sweat began to form on his head. The worst ideas about his mother developed in his mind. Then he walked out of the bedroom, and he turned the corner, and there she stood holding her chest. She ran to him and threw her arms around his neck, "Oh my dear son. What happened? You were late this morning, and I thought something must have happened to you. So, I walked out the back door to wait for you- to see if I could see you somehow through the trees in the back yard that leads to the street."

"Mama, I was only five minutes late due to traffic."

"Yes, but you broke our morning routine, and I thought something bad happened." "Why didn't you call?" she said.

"Again, I was five minutes late."

"I don't know what I would do if something happened to you."

"I'm right here, mom."

She grabbed her chest and let out a sigh of relief.

"Good, I will make a fresh pot of coffee, and we can begin our morning."

"Mom, there is nothing wrong with the coffee you made; we can drink it like it."

"Oh no, something could have gotten into the pot, and we could get sick. No worries, it will only take a few minutes while we wait on it. I must tell you about the fear for the day. You know that I enjoy sharing it with you. It's our thing; fear and morning coffee."

Minutes later, she returned with a fresh pot of coffee in hand and began speaking before she reached the table.

Yesterday, I was so afraid as I sat in the window…

Her voice grew faint as he remembered the first time he heard about fear; he was outside playing with friends with a ball and his mother after seeing the ball roll into the street and him chasing after it. She panicked, grabbed him by the arm, and into the house. She sat him in a chair and told him all about fear. How fear was all around him and that he had to be careful at play, at school, at home,

4

even while sleeping because fear lived in their house. As a young boy, he refused to play with the other kids for fear of something happening. Instead, he sat on the front porch with Mom and watched the others play. "Now, isn't this better than having to worry about something happening?

"Yes, mom, it is. Thank you for teaching me about fear.

Now, his chin resting in his hand as he watched his mom sitting across from him at the table sipping coffee as she continued to speak.

"So, I saw another form of fear walking up and down the street tormenting those that passed by, and I was afraid that fear would see me watching and come knocking at my door. You know, son, fear has lived in our home for as long as I could remember, and I do not need a stronger fear entering in this home." She continued.

"I agree, mom, and thank you so much for keeping me safe when I was younger by telling me all about fear. It stopped me from enjoying anything as I was growing up, and now as a man living with fear, I have settled for a lifeless than what I have seen."

"You know, mom, sometimes I wonder if there's something else in opposition to fear."

She picked up her cup and sipped twice before speaking.

"Oh, but there is, but don't you go talking about it for perfect love cast out fear, and I'm afraid fear might hear you and get upset and torment us."

He had heard enough of fear for the day. The truth is that he had feared for so long that it was all that he knew, but now, something was not right. He placed his hand on the table to rise and leave.

"Well, mom, it's time for me to get to work. Thank you for a morning coffee and fear. I will be cautious not to explore life or have any adventure, for fear is always there. I will see you when I get from work."

Mom stood up and walked her son to the door. She grabbed his arm and said, "Son, I thought that maybe you should move back home. That way, I don't have to worry about you. I will have your room ready for you today when you get off work.

"I guess it would be nice to make sure that you are not dealing with fear alone., but I have learned to live with the fear that you taught me, and I am comfortable. I do not want to disturb anything." The son spoke.

"Son, I am not asking you. I am telling you that you must come home. I went to the grocery store yesterday, and I was so paralyzed with fear that I could not leave, and you were working, so I stayed there for hours until I finally had someone to walk me to my car. I was afraid."

"Mama, I never want that to happen to you ever again, so I will move home into my old room."

"Thank you, and now we can be afraid, not only for morning coffee but dinner as well. You have made me so happy."

She clasped her hands together and praised her son for bowing down to fear.

FEAR IN OUR LIVES

It was Saturday morning, and the son was leaving his bedroom to meet mom for their usual coffee and fear. He stopped in mid-walk in the hallway and gripped his chest, and he could not move, his hands began to shake, he felt so afraid for his life. "Mom! He called out.

Mom came running around the corner – when she saw her son, she knew what was happening.

After calming him down – she asked him, "Sit down and let me tell you another part of fear. It comes in many forms – I learned early what those were and how to live with them from my family. I will tell you all about them." The son leaned in forward to listen.

Paralyzing Fear

Son, I have been startled by fear and could not move. I call this paralyzing fear because you stop breathing and become frozen in whatever you are doing.

"Really? -keep going." The son insisted.

"I have an aunt that received some disturbing news once, and fear gripped her and caused her to be paralyzed, and she lost consciousness."

"I never understood this as fear." The son replied.

She feared what would happen next. This paralyzing fear can also come when watching suspense or horror movies; the ones that have you sitting on the edge of your seat, holding your breath, afraid of the next move in the film. Suddenly you jerk, scream or clench your fists; Fear had made its entrance into her life.

The son's face looked astonished.

"Oh, don't worry about that- we as a family are known, fearful people. We expect fear in our lives."

"I have another relative that was home alone; there was a storm that night, and the lights flicker. She heard a creaking sound from another room in the house. She paused, and then she heard a door close. Her entire body tensed up into a paralyzing stance while she anticipated the next move to make. This paralyzing fear had taken over her body and now played tricks with her mind. She remembers all sorts of images from watching movies, hearing stories from others, and even her life experiences were wreaking havoc on her thoughts. The reality is that an open window in the next room had enabled a strong wind from the storm to come through and close the door."

The son continued to listen, "tell me more, Mom."

Octopus Fear

"Well, another relative received a phone call about bad news. She grabbed her chest and asked, "what happened?" This sudden but forceful spirit of fear forced its way in by suspicion of what happened. I call it the octopus fear because that is what this feels like when it enters. It comes suddenly and causes you to grab your chest, and you can feel the gripping pain."

"This is all interesting, mom- I guess I need to know all about fear if I have to live with it for the rest of my life."

"Okay, well, I will continue to teach you all about it.

Running Fear

"What I call the running fear is only running away from things and people that you don't want to face for fear of hurt, fear that it will happen again- fear of failure, or fear of success. It has kept our family for generations from prospering in our finances, relationships, and even advancement in business. And fear has stopped our family from making logical decisions for our lives."

"Mom, all of this reminds me of the business idea that I had a few years ago, but I would not move forward on it for fear of failure. Fear stopped me from pursuing the idea because I didn't want to fail. I just kept telling myself that I needed to research a little bit more. After a while, I just settled for the safe route and continued working for a company. I still think about that idea from time to time, but I know that as long as fear lives in our home, it will never become anything. Mom, I wish there was something that I could do to get rid of fear."

She stands up and rushes over to her son, takes one finger, and puts it over his lips. "I told you to stop talking like that-we don't want Fear to hear us and torment us more. Just learn to live with it and move on with your comfortable life."

"Son, please tell me you will let this go."

"Okay, mom, I will let it go for now."

"But I have one question, Mom, where did you learn to fear?

"How much time do you have, son? That's a long story of our generations of fear- my mother, grandmother, and great-grandmother. As far back as we can remember."

"I'm free all day- I need to know where this started."

"I had to be about ten years old. I woke up to a loud sound in the middle of the night with a paralyzing fear. I yelled out, what is your name? I heard nothing, so I went back to sleep after my mom came in and calmed me down."

"Mom said before leaving the room. "It's okay, darling – it's just fear, go back to sleep."

"The next day I was watching a movie about a princess with a special power."

"It was the scene where the young princess had these powers that she and her sister enjoyed. One night she mistakenly strikes her younger sister with her powers, and the parents take her to the love experts to ensure she is okay. They told the parents that the child would need to learn to use her powers or fear would be her greatest enemy. They showed a vision of fear tormenting the young princess and then devouring her. She watched the image and was immediately stricken with fear of using the powers that once gave her such great joy and pleasure.

That's it! I yelled. And now, I had a name. I ran to tell mom while she was making dinner. I know why I feel afraid all the time. Its name is Fear!"

"My mom smiled and spoke."

"Yes, darling, we know what the name is our family has always known."

SILENT TESTIMONY

"Son, I asked her the same thing that you are asking me about fear."

"What's that, mom?"

"I asked if anyone in our family has gotten rid of fear."

"Well, what did she say?"

"She was hesitant before she shared a story

of her sister. She conquered fear with faith and love, but when all of the other family members heard of this- they bombarded her with so much fear – day and night that she became fearful again and never spoke of her testimony of defeating fear."

"Which aunt is this, mom?"

"Son, I know what you are thinking, and I'm telling you to let it go."

The son was still perplexed that Fear could be defeated. He rose from the table and left the room.

Close the Door on Fear

Months had passed, and mother and son continued their morning coffee with a dose of fear. But now, she noticed that something had changed with her son. He was no longer attentive to the fearful conversations. He was often seen drifting off alone to be on the phone leaving home for hours unaccounted for. All of this made his mom extremely afraid, for she feared the worst. So, she had to add more fear to get him back into submission.

The following day of their coffee date, she babbled with much fear.

"Son, I need you to know that the fear that we are used to has grown, and now we must fear even more, which means maybe you should quit your job so that you can be home with me all day."

"No, ma'am, nothing's wrong. I wanted to speak with you. Remember when I asked you months ago about something in opposition to fear? Well, I found it, and I have been spending time with her."

"I knew it - now I'm fearing the worst. You are leaving."

"Mom, no, I'm not leaving. I met a beautiful young lady, and her name is Love. That's who I have been spending time with."

"I want you to meet her, she is beautiful, and everything fear is not."

Mom grabbed her chest and began breathing heavily.

"Oh, don't you dare bring Love into this house."

"Mama, you will love her."

"No, mom stood up and walked away-No! No! No!

"I know that you have only known Fear, but you must meet Love." He whispered as she walked away.

Weeks later.

Mom was sitting on the couch watching the fear box when she heard her son's usual knock then heard him unlocking the door with his key. She had no reason to fear because she knew that it was him, he walked in the door on a Friday night as usual, but this time someone followed closely behind him. His mom could not see who it was, but she could smell her sweet floral scent floating through; interrupting the smell of fear in the atmosphere, she swayed her dress from left to right and walked right up to his mom and hugged her with the biggest, warmest hug that she could muster up.

"Hi, I have heard everything about you. My name is Love, and I'm crazy about your son." She smiled with the brightest smile mom had seen.

Mom – barely embraced Love back – but instead asked the son to meet her in the next room.

"Son, are you sure about this Love person. I mean, I'm afraid that she will hurt you or leave you. You must get her out of here. I felt something when she hugged me. I'm telling you it's not right to have Love here."

"Mom, I'm sure about Love, she is fantastic- she has already been talking to me about love, and I don't think we have to fear any longer. And what you felt when you hugged her is love, not fear."

"Fear is all that we have ever known, and if I let it go, then what will we have?" mom spoke.

"I told you that fear comes in many forms- maybe she is fear pretending to be Love- Oh, how I wish that she is Fear – may a new fear that we can get used to."

"I think I want to marry her …. the words were slow and steady."

This made mom fear even more at the thought of her son leaving to be with Love –

no way she could be alone. She needed him to share the fear. It was their thing.

"Spending time with LOVE has already changed your thinking, son. You no longer listen and fear with me; now, you challenge everything that I say about fear. I'm afraid that she will leave you and hurt you. Remember how the others came along and I told you they would leave you – and they did. This will be the same, maybe even worst. Please - I beg you to let Love go -so that we can go back to our daily routine of coffee and fear – dinner and fear."

More time had passed, and now the son had married Love.

Mom stood face to face with him after the wedding ceremony.

"Son, I'm sorry that I could not stop you from marrying Love."

"Mom, I love her, and I love you, but I must move on to a new life with Love. I have lived with fear in our home all my life."

Mom thought about what the son was telling her, and she had to do something quickly, I know she thought. I must call all the other relatives to ask them to come over soon- just like they did with my aunt that conquered fear. They will indeed pour so much fear into him that he will leave Love for good, and if that does not work- then I must pretend to like love so that my son does not leave home."

Just before the couple was about to leave for their honeymoon, Mom pulled her son to the side – out of earshot of Love.

"Son, I think that I like Love, now and want the two of you to move into the home with me as well."

The son exhaled at the thought. It would be difficult to leave what he had known for so long, but he wanted more. He stood perplexed about the decision. Then he spoke.

"Mom, I don't think that's a good idea. We must leave for our adventure."

"Son, I can't live alone with fear - I must have someone to fear with me. Please rethink this moving thing."

Love overheard the conversation and spoke.

" I don't mind living with your mom for a little bit to help her overcome fear."

Mom's facial expression changed to disgust.

"Oh, I don't need help getting rid of fear – it has been with me all of my life as well. I'm comfortable with it."

Love just smiled and knew things would be different with her in the home.

Some time had passed, and after watching and listening to the son and his mom with their morning coffee and fear. Love asked, "May I join you this morning and every morning for your coffee and chat?"

Mom looked at the son and blurted out.

"Love, I agreed to let you live here with my son, but I didn't know that you would want to interrupt our routine. I thought that you would even join us in coffee and fear. "

"Oh, it is impossible for me to fear- I'm love."

Mom looked confused because she had never had love in her home.

"Mom, I want to tell you that I want Love to join us with our morning coffee. I'm no longer interested in fear talking. I have learned so much by spending time with Love, and I think that you should spend time with her as well."

Mom began to breathe faster- I think I'm fearful of all of this change. Why would you go and do this to our lives? We were so comfortable living with fear, and now I have been tormented every night by fear because Love is here in our home."

"And why does she just stand there listening to us instead of joining our coffee and fear chat?"

She grew angry at the thought of Love in her home.

"Because Love has to be invited, unlike fear who will take over and move in without asking."

He saw the distress that the conversation was causing his mom, so he knew that she needed Love more than ever.

"If you want us to continue to live here with you, then Love has to join us in the mornings before we leave for work."

Tears began to form, and mom started breathing heavily again, gripping her chest, and being paralyzed with fear.

The son waves for Love to join. She puts her hand on her mother -in -law shoulder, and instantly mom calms down and is overwhelmed with love.

She looks at Love and says, "how did you do that? What was that?"

Love smiled and said, "It was love that you felt."

Then there was a knock at the door. The son opened it by asking who it was? He heard nothing from the other side and slightly opened the door to see outside. They pushed the door open, and several people came rushing in it was the family of fear. They grabbed the son and shoved him into a corner. "We heard you have encountered Love – well, we are here to get fear back into you for good." Someone shouted.

"Grab his feet, "another one yelled.

The son's eyes widened; he had never seen fear so aggressive. He was beginning to be more afraid. He looked at Love and motioned to help.

Love smiled and stepped towards the son and grabbed his hand. "Who is she? We will make her fear as well." A family member yelled out.

"It's my wife Love." When the feared family heard this, they all started to back off, saying "Oh, we did know you were married to Love."

They began one by one to walk towards the door to leave.

"There's nothing we can do here- it's too late- he has already married Love which means it's in his heart. Unlike our other relative who conquered it, but she was married to it; therefore, it was easier for us to come back into her life."

Without another further word- they ran out the door and slammed it shut.

The son looked at Love and said, "I'm so happy that I found you and that you were here; otherwise, I would have surely been overtaken by fear again."

"Thank you for inviting me into your life." Love spoke.

Mama was intrigued by Love and spoke.

"Tell me all about you."

"I will make some fresh coffee for us- give me just a second."

So, now, Mama, son, and Love sat down for morning coffee and a dose of love, instead of fear.

Overcoming the Spirit of Fear

Weeks later, Love asked if someone else could join the morning chat. She saw that mom had grown interested in love and needed more encouragement. Fear had been with her for so long that it was harder for her to release it without doubting and fear that something bad would happen.

The son had never met her sister because although he had grown in love, he was still with his mom and Fear, now was a better time for the family to meet her.

"Sure," he said.

Moments later a knock at the door came, and Love asked if she may answer it.

"Absolutely," mom said. "You are welcome to open the door and invite anyone into our home."

Love walked to the door, opened it, and in walked a woman just as beautiful as she was. "Everyone, meet my sister Faith."

Gaining Faith and Love

"Now, we have Faith and Love in our home; that would surely kick fear out. The son spoke.

"Yes, Faith spoke- now may we pray?"

"Yes, mom exclaimed."

They all gathered around and held hands. Faith spoke:

Heavenly Father, in the name of Jesus, I ask for forgiveness for inviting fear into our lives and our home. I come to you in faith, believing in your love and protection for me and all that concerns me. I thank you for giving us the spirit of power, love, and a sound mind to conquer the spirit of fear. I trust you and close the door on the spirit of fear in my life and all that concerns me. In Jesus' name, I pray with thanksgiving.

Amen.

The morning routine now consists of Mama, son, Love, and Faith regularly stopping by each morning. Soon when their love and knowledge had grown, she would be able to move in, but right now, their faith was still too small, fear still occupied a small space in her mind. Therefore, Faith was invited each morning instead.

During one of their morning chats, mom said without thinking.

"Oh, guys, have a seat before Faith arrives. I must pour you coffee and give you a dose of fear to take along the day with you.

But love stops her after a distressed look on her face. "Oh, love casts out fear- we must not carry fear with us throughout our day."

Mama immediately stopped and felt a little embarrassed. She chuckled and spoke. "Oh guys, I'm sorry about that. It is just so hard to get rid of a habit of fear."

Love spoke, "it takes practice and choosing our thoughts daily, or the sneaky fear will try to come back. Remember that."

"A huge smile came across mom's face. Tears poured from her eyes as they hugged. I never thought this moment would ever be possible in my life or to see my son set free from fear. I don't remember the last time that I saw fear since you been here, Love."

Mom enjoyed having Love in the house – and a dose of Faith daily. She didn't know when fear had left, just that it was gone. Or it just wasn't magnified as much as before.

Faith arrived and joined her sister Love in the morning chat. Love knew that she had to talk more about Faith; while she was here in the room, she had not been fully activated because of a lack of knowledge. Mom and son needed to know how to use Faith and Love, or fear would try to return.

"Let's talk about the power of Faith and trusting God. Your instructions are in the Bible for you to follow in moments of weakness.

Love gave mom and son a Bible and said turn to Proverbs 3:5 "Trust in the Lord with all thine heart and lean not unto thine own understanding." When fear comes to your mind.

"How can you trust in God when you don't know what to trust in Him?" Mom spoke.

"So glad you asked by reading and studying His Word and by spending time in prayer and worship to hear what He says to you personally. When you know who you are in Christ, it will help you in gaining faith and love."

Faith is just trusting in the love that God has for you. You cannot think of negative or fearful things when you have the mind of Christ. Guard yourself against the attacks of the enemy trying to come into that space where it was rejected.

God loves you as a believer in His son Jesus Christ who went to the cross of human death and took your sins with him. Fear will make you believe that you are alone, and no help is available. You have invisible help to fight against the things that you can't see. Faith will help you to believe that you are not alone against fear. When you began to see, feel, hear fear- bring it down out of your mind with prayer daily until it is gone."

"Which prayer, Mom asked?"

"2 Corinthians 10:3-5 (KJV). "Casting down imaginations, and every high thing that exalted itself against the knowledge of God and bringing into captivity every thought to the obedience of Christ" Love spoke.

Pray but keep a watchful eye for fear.

"What do you mean, keep a watchful eye for fear?" Mom spoke.

"You shall see in the coming days for yourself, surely as you been increasing in faith and love fear will attempt its return to what he calls his home." Love spoke and faith smiled.

Increasing your faith

A few nights later while sleeping, mom was awakened by the front door that opened and closed. She jumped out of bed and walked towards the door, and behold, it was fear. "I'm home!" He shouted.

"No, she shouted louder. "You no longer live here."

"But I thought that you just needed time – and that I could return."

"No! she continued to shout, get out of here, fear."

Fear laughed at the request and shoved her aside. I'm not asking you to invite me inside. Who do you think that I am Love?"

"I have seen what it feels like without you, and I like it." Mom shouted.

"But I thought this was my home- I have been with you – I mean your family for so long…generations."

"Stop talking and get out you will not convince me to let you stay." "Get out." She continued to shout.

But fear did not budge.

You don't have enough power to send me away- for good- only one way that will happen, and your family generation has not mastered that.

So, step aside and let me in. I have a great deal of fear to give you. This time, I will make sure that you don't go talking this crazy talk about faith or love. Oh, you thought I didn't know that you were trying to increase your confidence to get rid of me for good.? That's why I came at night when your guards were down, and I could get you alone. I know that your son and Love are out of town for the weekend."

Mom's face lit up, and she began to pray asking for faith and love to return to her home to help fight against fear. She began calling on her help.

They both appeared at the door, mom saw them, but fear didn't. He continued to ramble on and on about where he would live in her home.

Mom opened the door wider and yelled, get out fear in Jesus Christ's name and never return to my home or my son's or even my future generations to come. I repent forever letting you in my life. I cast you out in the name, power, and authority of Jesus Christ, the Messiah!

Just like that, both faith and love came around the corner and stood with Mom, and fear trembled and said, "Oh, I see that you figured it out.

I'm out of here! And you don't have to worry about me coming around here anymore.

Fear paused- turned around and spoke.

"But then again, I might walk past your home from time to time to see if you still have faith and love in here. If not, I'm warning you I will return with not just fear, but I will bring seven more spirits like procrastination, pride, doubt, shame, lust, greed, and poverty along with me."

"Oh, no need to think about coming back here- faith and love will live here forever."

Faith stood to mom left and love to her right.

Fear took one more look and then fled out the door.

Faith and Love spoke in unison-"you will need to spend more time with us to increase your faith and love- because fear is correct if you leave a crack open, it will try to come back now, let's repent for your ancestors that allowed fear to arrive."

Faith spoke. "Increasing your faith is not something that happens overnight. It will require you to be active in speaking and declaring the word of God over all that concerns you. Take some time daily and learn that new scripture about faith that I gave you. Study the scripture to get a deep meaning to make it personal to you.

The following morning of coffee and a dose of love and faith, the son spoke.

They sipped coffee and exchanged grateful smiles amongst each other.

"Mom, I want to share something that I have been reading with you. It's a story in the book of Joshua."

BELIEVING GOD PROMISE

He continued- "In the Bible, Moses was ordered by the Lord to send men to explore the land of Canaan that He would give to the Israelites. Moses sent one man from each tribe, twelve in all. The men were to observe the people's weaknesses and their strengths. Whether they were strong or weak, did they have walls, or were they unprotected? Is it fertile or poor? They needed to know how to proceed with the attack upon the impending people in the land. When the men returned to report the finding, the report was filled with fear because the people were powerful, and the land was overflowing with milk and honey. They described the people as giants against them. The others that listened became fearful and wanted to return to slavery in Egypt!"

"At this moment, the act of being fearless rises in Caleb against what he saw in the land that they were to conquer. The others feared because what they were to come up against seemed greater than themselves, and they suddenly felt defeated, but God had ordered their steps to conquer the land and overtake the people. And then Caleb spoke in boldness against fear in Number: 13:30 30 But Caleb quieted the people before Moses and said, "Let us go up at once and occupy it, for we are well able to overcome it." I believe that Caleb's fearlessness was in the knowledge that God would indeed be with them. He knew that the power that sent them would be greater than what the natural eye could see— believing in the promise made Caleb fearless for the task.

I said of that mom to tell you that now that I have increased in Faith and Love, I have been busy working on that idea that fear kept me from pursuing – therefore, I will be on my new adventure to follow a life without tormenting fear because I know that God has given the vision to build, and He will be with me even though it looks scary where I'm going- because of the unknown. I know that I will encounter fear along the way, but I will never let it stop me in my life ever again."

"Also, Mom I'm very proud of you for last night you showed much faith in believing in your invisible help against fear- that's why faith and love showed up."

"I'm so happy for you, son, and thank you for bringing both into our family. I will be forever grateful. Go and live your life, and I will do the same. I called your father and told him to come back home. I was so afraid that he would leave that I kicked him out. He has never stopped calling and pursuing me. He said he would pray and wait on me to get rid of that fear."

The son stood to hug his mom.

"Yes, mom, that sounds great."

Faith and Love joined in, and another knock was at the door. Mom thought it was fear returning. She said. "I got this one."

She opened the door, ready to fight fear but her husband stood there and embraced her. "I Love You, dear." He spoke.

"I love you too, my wonderful husband."

Come inside and meet…

"Hello, Faith and Love."

"Wait, you know them?" Mom spoke.

"Yes, we met your husband when you kicked him out. He has been praying and covering you and your son daily, asking that we, Faith and Love visit."

"So, why didn't you tell me earlier?" Mom spoke.

"You had to accept us for yourself – through wisdom and knowledge." "Understood." Mom said.

Love spoke: "Let me give you some Bible scriptures that you will need to use against fear the next time it thinks about coming around. It will also keep both Faith and Love in your home and in your heart. Oh Yea, if you haven't noticed, Peace is here as well.

FAITH
BIBLE
VERSES

Bible Verses About Fear – It's a good thing to read scriptures that can encourage you on topics relating to fighting against fear. It will increase your Christian faith. Write them down and post them in your car, near your bed so that it's the first thing you see when you get up in the morning and the last thing you see at night. Anyplace that will cause you to remember them.

Isaiah 35:4

Four say to those with fearful hearts, "Be strong, do not fear; your God will come, he will come with a vengeance; with divine retribution, he will come to save you."

John 14:27

27 Peace I leave with you; my peace I give you. I do not give to you as the world gives. Do not let your hearts be troubled and do not be afraid.

Joshua 1:9

9 Have I not commanded you? Be strong and courageous. Do not be afraid; do not be discouraged, for the LORD, your God will be with you wherever you go."

Matthew 6:34

34 Therefore do not worry about tomorrow, for tomorrow will worry about itself. Each day has enough trouble of its own.

Isaiah 43:1

1 But now, this is what the LORD says— he who created you, Jacob, he who formed you, Israel: "Do not fear, for I have redeemed you; I have summoned you by name; you are mine.

Psalm 23:4

4 Even though I walk through the darkest valley, I will fear no evil, for you are with me; your rod and your staff, they comfort me.

Psalm 34:4

4 I sought the LORD, and he answered me; he delivered me from all my fears.

Psalm 94:19

19 When anxiety was great within me, your consolation brought me joy.

Romans 8:38-39

38 For I am convinced that neither death nor life, neither angels nor demons, neither the present nor the future, nor any powers, 39 neither height nor depth, nor anything else in all creation, will be able to separate us from the love of God that is in Christ Jesus our Lord.

Psalm 27:1

1 The LORD is my light and my salvation— whom shall I fear? The LORD is the stronghold of my life— of whom shall I be afraid?

1 Peter 5:6-7

6 Humble yourselves, therefore, under God's mighty hand, that he may lift you in due time. 7 Cast all your anxiety on him because he cares for you.

Psalm 118:6

6 The LORD is with me; I will not be afraid. What can mere mortals do to me?

2 Timothy 1:7

7 For the spirit God gave us does not make us timid, but gives us power, love, and self-discipline.

Psalm 115:11

11 You who fear him, trust in the LORD— he is their help and shield.

Psalm 103:17

17 But from everlasting to everlasting the LORD's love is with those who fear him, and his righteousness with their children's children—

Psalm 112:1

1 Praise the LORD. Blessed are those who fear the LORD, who find great delight in his commands.

Deuteronomy 31:6
6 Be strong and courageous. Do not be afraid or terrified because of them, for the LORD your God goes with you; he will never
leave you nor forsake you."

1 Chronicles 28:20
20 David also said to Solomon his son, "Be strong and courageous, and do the work. Do not be afraid or discouraged, for the LORD God, my God, is with you. He will not fail you or forsake you until all the work for the service of the temple of the LORD is finished.
Psalm 56:3-4

3 When I am afraid, I put my trust in you. 4 In God, whose word I praise— in God I trust and am not afraid. What can mere mortals do to me?

Isaiah 41:10

10 So do not fear, for I am with you; do not be dismayed, for I am your God. I will strengthen you and help you; I will uphold you with my righteous right hand.

Isaiah 41:13

13 For I am the LORD your God who takes hold of your right hand and says to you, Do not fear; I will help you.

Isaiah 54:4

4 "Do not be afraid; you will not be put to shame. Do not fear disgrace; you will not be humiliated. You will forget the shame of your youth and remember no more the reproach of your widowhood.

Matthew 10:28

28 Do not be afraid of those who kill the body but cannot kill the soul. Rather, be afraid of the One who can destroy both soul and body in hell.

Romans 8:15

15 The spirit you received does not make you slaves, so that you live in fear again;

rather, the spirit you received brought about your adoption to sonship. And by him we cry, "Abba, Father."

1 Corinthians 16:13

13 Be on your guard; stand firm in the faith; be courageous; be strong.

Hebrews 13:5-6

5 Keep your lives free from the love of money and be content with what you have, because God has said, "Never will I leave you; never will I forsake you." 6 So we say with confidence, "The Lord is my helper; I will not
be afraid. What can mere mortals do to me?"

1 Peter 3:13-14

13 Who is going to harm you if you are eager to do good? 14 But even if you should suffer for what is right, you are blessed. "Do not fear their threats; do not be frightened."

1 John 4:18

18 There is no fear in love. But perfect love drives out fear, because fear has to do with punishment. The one who fears is not made perfect in love.

TAMBEARA WATKINS

ABOUT THE AUTHOR

Tambeara Watkins was born and raised in Atlanta Georgia. She enjoys outdoor activities and design.

CPSIA information can be obtained
at www.ICGtesting.com
Printed in the USA
LVHW050918f20422
715893LV00013B/2237